Date Due

DATE DUE

Demco, Inc. 38-293

O Canada!

For
Clare Ruthven Barclay
and her grandchildren

O CANADA!

ISABEL BARCLAY

Illustrated by Cécile Gagnon

DOUBLEDAY & COMPANY, INC.,
GARDEN CITY, NEW YORK

J
971
B

ACKNOWLEDGMENTS

Among those who have helped me with criticism and suggestions I am especially indebted to Dr. W. E. Taylor, Department of Anthropology, National Museum of Canada, Professor J. I. Cooper, Department of History, McGill University, and Miss Katherine Lamont, Headmistress of The Study, Montreal.

I am also very grateful to the 1962–63 class of Upper A. at The Study, who first listened to this story and helped in more ways than they knew.

Montreal

ISABEL BARCLAY

2-12-65

Library of Congress Catalog Card Number 64–12591
Text Copyright © 1964 by Isabel Barclay Dobell
Illustrations Copyright © 1964 by Cécile Gagnon

O Canada

Once upon a time, long ago, nobody lived in Canada. There were animals and birds in the forests and on the plains and among the mountains. There were fish in the rivers and lakes and streams and in the seas, but there were no people.

For millions of years there were no people anywhere in North America. Then the first men came. They came across a strip of land that once made a pathway in the north between Asia and America. They probably came to hunt the animals whose skins they used for clothes and whose flesh they used for food.

These people all came from Asia but they were not all

5

alike nor did they all come at once. They kept coming in small numbers for thousands and thousands of years, and when they came they stayed.

Some of them settled along the Pacific coast.

Some wandered down the warm valleys behind the Rocky Mountains until they came to Mexico and South America.

Some settled on the edge of the prairies.

Others wandered first south and then north until they came to the eastern woodlands and the shores of the Atlantic Ocean.

There were still others who stayed in the arctic and learned to live by the frozen seas. These were the Eskimo, and their descendants are still there.

All these early people had different shades of brown skin and straight black hair and dark brown eyes, but they did not look alike, or speak the same language, or have the same customs. We call them INDIANS because of a mistake made nearly five hundred years ago. The first Europeans to reach America thought they had found India and so they called the people living there INDIANS and that is what they have been called ever since. The Eskimo and the Indians never had a name for themselves. They simply called themselves THE PEOPLE.

The People of the Arctic

The Eskimo who lived in the arctic had pale brown skin, slanting eyes, and straight dark hair. They were not tall but they were very strong and great hunters. They hunted many animals, especially the seals and walrus that lived in the ocean and the polar bears and caribou that lived on the land.

During the winter, which in the arctic lasts half the year, the Eskimo lived in snow houses. These houses were made out of blocks of snow.

During the summer the Eskimo lived in tents made of animal skins.

In winter they travelled by dog sled or on foot.

In summer they went on foot or in their kayaks and umiaks. These are sealskin boats. The Eskimo made their boats from sealskin because trees do not grow in the arctic. The only wood the Eskimo had was the driftwood that floated down the rivers from places farther south where it was warm enough for trees to grow.

The Eskimo were Stone Age men. That is to say they lived without the discovery of metals and so most of their

7

tools and weapons were made of stone. Even their arrow-heads were pieces of chipped flint and their lamps were hollowed stones filled with seal or whale oil.

Like most Stone Age people the Eskimo lived in tribes. In each tribe were several families. The men and boys did the hunting and fishing. Hunting was hard and dangerous. Sometimes the Eskimo had to travel many miles before they found game.

The women cooked and sewed and cured the skins of the animals caught in the hunt.

This was done by scraping the skins with sharp stone scrapers and then stretching them on frames to dry. When they were dry, the women cut the skins with stone knives, then sewed the pieces together with bone needles and thread made of sinew.

The Eskimo believed in Good and Bad Spirits. The Good Spirits were the Spirits of their ancestors and the Bad Spirits the Beings who ruled the Earth and Air. The Eskimo made offerings to the Good Spirits and did their best to please the Bad Spirits, or else to frighten them away by shouting and cracking dog whips and making a great noise whenever they thought a Bad Spirit was about. But the Spirits of the Wind and the Sea and the Cold are not easily frightened and so the Eskimo had to learn to live with them as best they could.

The Eskimo were a friendly people. They did not waste their strength and skill fighting. It took all their strength and skill just to keep alive on the edge of the cold arctic seas.

The People of the Eastern Woodlands

The part of Canada that lies between the Great Lakes and the Atlantic Ocean is a land of woods and hills and lakes and rivers and streams. These are the Eastern Woodlands and here long ago lived the Woodland peoples. There were many different Woodland Indians.

The Beothuk lived in Newfoundland.

The Algonkians lived in Quebec and Labrador, and in what is now Nova Scotia and New Brunswick and Prince Edward Island and the north shore of the St. Lawrence River.

The Iroquois lived along the south shore of the St. Lawrence River and beside Lake Ontario and Lake Erie in parts of the country that now belong to the United States.

Other Algonkian people lived along the Ottawa River, while the Hurons lived in southern Ontario and round about Lake Huron, and the Cree lived among the lakes and woods that stretch from the west side of the Great Lakes to the Prairies.

Life was easier for the Woodland people than it was for the people of the arctic. In the parts of Canada where *they* lived, the sun shone all the year, the woods were filled with game and the lakes and rivers with fish.

Wild berries grew in the clearings and there were shellfish on the shore.

The Woodland Indians hunted moose and caribou and deer, and each tribe had its own hunting grounds.

All the Woodland people used skins to make their clothing, but not to make their dwellings. They lived in wigwams made of bark, or long houses that were built with slabs of bark and saplings.

They used bark to make canoes and baskets.

Some of the Woodland Indians painted their clothes and baskets with bright designs, or embroidered them with moose hair and porcupine quills. They made their dyes from plants and berries.

The Woodland Indians, like other people of the Stone Age, knew how to make fire but they did not know how to make wheels. When they travelled they had to carry their belongings on their backs or drag them over the snow on toboggans.

They used snowshoes to walk in the deep snow.

In summer travelling was easier because they could paddle along the lakes and rivers.

Birch bark canoes were made from the bark of the white birch tree. First the bark was cut from the tree in such a way that it came off all in one piece.

Then cedar branches were bent into the right shape and fastened to a frame.

The branches were covered with the birch bark and the bark and branches were lashed with roots and glued with gum from the evergreens.

These birch bark canoes were so light a man could carry one on his back. At the same time they were so strong a single canoe held many men.

When they made war, the Woodland Indians used bows and arrows, spears, and clubs. These weapons were made of wood and stone or bone. But mostly they were tipped with stone.

Many of the Woodland people depended on farming as well as on hunting and fishing for their food. The Iroquois were the best farmers. They lived in villages surrounded by high, spiked wooden fences. In each village there were a number of long houses. Several families lived in a long house. Each family had its own place and its own fire. The fires were built down the center of the long house and the smoke escaped through holes in the roof.

Outside the village walls were the fields where the Iroquois grew their crops. The women did all the work in the fields. They planted corn, beans, squash, pumpkins, and bright yellow sunflowers. Their tools were very simple. A hoe was made by fastening a sharp stone or clamshell to the end of a stick. They also used a pointed stick to dig holes for their seeds.

When the corn was ripe the women pounded it in a hollow log to make corn meal.

The Iroquois used hollow logs for all sorts of things. They even used them to make boats. They did not always have bark canoes like the Algonkians because very few birch trees grew in their part of the country. They often had hollow log boats, or dugouts, made from elm logs. They hollowed logs by burning them along one side and chipping out the burned wood.

The Woodland Indians made most of their clothes from deerskin. In summer the men wore only breechclouts and the women skirts. The children wore no clothes at all.

In winter the men and women and children wore deerskin skirts and leggings. They also had fur caps and mittens and fur-lined moccasins. When it was very, very cold they wrapped themselves in capes of beaver skin.

The mothers carried their papooses in cradleboards on their backs.

The Woodland Indians had exciting feasts and festivals. In the fall when the crops were ripe they had a Harvest Festival. There were other festivals in the winter and spring and summer. At these festivals everybody danced and sang and made long speeches and stuffed themselves with food.

All the people of the Eastern Woodlands believed in a Great Spirit. They said it was He who had made the world and all the people and animals in it. The Woodland Indians believed there were spirits in all things—in the trees and birds and fish and animals, as well as in themselves and in the wind and the rain.

The People of the Plains

In what are now the provinces of Manitoba and Saskatchewan and Alberta, that is, in the land that lies between the Eastern Woodlands and the Rocky Mountains, are the Great Plains or Prairies as they are called in Canada. Here the buffalo roamed in tremendous herds, and here lived the Plains Indians—the Blackfoot, the Assiniboine, the Sarcee, and the Sioux.

These people depended on the buffalo for almost everything. They used his flesh for food, his skin for clothing, and his horns and bones for weapons and tools.

They even used buffalo skins to make their boats and their tents or tepees, because they lived in an almost treeless land.

The Plains Indians learned to make a very nourishing food from dried buffalo meat. First the women cut the meat in strips and hung it on a pole over a fire to dry. When it was dry they pounded it with mallets and mixed it into a

paste with melted buffalo fat and crushed wild berries. Then
they shaped the paste into cakes and baked the cakes on hot
stones. This was called PEMMICAN and later it became as use-
ful to the white man as it was to the Plains People.

The boats of the Plains Indians were round. They were
made of bent willow saplings and covered with buffalo hide.
These round boats were light and strong and could be easily
carried. The Plains Indians used their boats to cross the
great rivers that flowed through the prairies—the Red, the
Peace, and the North and South Saskatchewan, though of
course in those days these rivers had other names.

Wherever the buffalo herds roamed the Plains Indians
followed.

In the beginning the Indians who lived on the Great Plains had to follow the buffalo on foot for they had only dogs for beasts of burden. The dog was the only animal the Eskimo and Indians ever tamed. After the white men came to North America there were horses. The horses made great changes in the lives of the Plains Indians. Before the coming of the horses the Plains Indians lived in round earth lodges on the edge of the prairies. Here the women and children stayed to look after the gardens while the men went hunting. The men hunted most of the year. In the fall they returned to the earth lodges and their families but only for a little while.

After there were horses on the Plains living was easier. The Plains Indians began to give up their earth lodges and gardens to spend most of their lives following the buffalo herds.

The Plains Indians hunted buffalo in different ways. Sometimes the buffalo were driven over cliffs to be killed by the fall.

Sometimes the Indians disguised themselves in wolfskins and crept along the ground until they were near enough to the animals to use their bows and arrows.

Once they had horses they hunted on horseback.

The Plains Indians made headdresses and war bonnets out of eagle feathers, and ornaments out of claws and bones.

Because they moved about so much, the Plains Indians liked to make things that were easy to carry. When they travelled from one camping ground to another they used their tepees like carts. They did this by binding the tepee poles into a V and tying a leather harness between the poles. This is a TRAVOIS. The Plains Indians first had dog travois and then horse travois.

The Plains Indians were great warriors and delighted to tell stories about their brave deeds. Nearly all of their feasts and festivals had to do with buffalo hunting or making war.

The People of the North West Coast

In the land between the Rocky Mountains and the Pacific Ocean there are mighty forests. Here, the fir and cedar trees grow taller than anywhere else in the world. Great rivers rush down from the mountains to the sea. The coast is filled with bays and inlets and there are many islands. Here, long ago, lived the Indians of the North West Coast— the Tlinkit, the Nootka, the Kwakiutl and the Haida.

These people had a much easier life than the people of the Plains or the Eastern Woodlands. Almost everything they needed was close at hand for almost everything they needed came from the giant trees and the sea.

The Indians of the North West Coast did not have to plant crops. Near the Pacific Ocean the climate is mild and fruit and berries grow in the woods all the year round.

The North West Coast Indians hunted the great sea ani-

mals—seals and whales and porpoises and sea otters. But their favourite food was salmon.

Their tools and weapons were made of slate and wood and the copper they found in the rocks.

They made their clothes out of coarse cloth. This cloth was woven from the bark of cedar trees and wool from the coats of Rocky Mountain sheep.

They made their houses out of planks cut from the giant trees. The houses stood in rows along the edge of the beaches.

The canoes of the North West Coast Indians were made of hollow logs. They had canoes of many sizes. The smallest were just big enough for two people while the largest could hold as many as fifty. The larger canoes were used to hunt sea animals and to travel up and down the coast. Few things were as important to the people of the North West Coast as their seagoing canoes.

The North West Coast Indians knew many ways to hunt and fish. They caught salmon by spearing them with harpoons; or trapping them in weirs; or catching them in nets made of vines.

They learned how to dry and smoke meat and fish. This meant they always had food on hand and hardly ever had to worry about being hungry.

The people of the North West Coast made all sorts of beautiful things.

They were excellent carpenters and wood carvers. They made beautifully carved wooden boxes and dishes and shields and helmets. They made spoons out of animal horns, and carved them too. They liked to decorate everything they owned, even the wooden paddles for their seagoing canoes.

They wove blankets of cedar bark and mountain sheep's wool in black and shades of soft blue, yellow, and green.

The North West Coast Indians made totem poles. Some totem poles were small and carved from slate or wood. Some were enormous and made from the trunks of trees. The totem poles were carved with figures of beasts and birds. The people of the North West Coast believed they were descended from beasts and birds and the carvings on their totem poles sometimes told the history of their families.

The North West Coast people were very proud and every man liked to be thought richer than his neighbour. Sometimes, to show how rich he was, a chief would destroy his possessions. He might break a copper ornament and throw the pieces away, or hack a big canoe into bits, as if to say: "See how rich and powerful I am! I can even afford to destroy my most precious things."

Sometimes he would hold a feast and give valuable presents to all his guests. These feasts were called POTLATCHES.

Many of the most beautiful things the North West Coast Indians made were for the chiefs to give as presents at the potlatches.

The North West Coast Indians believed in a number of spirits, but especially the spirits of the beasts and birds they thought were their ancestors.

At their feasts and festivals they loved to act and to tell stories about these creatures.

The Coming of the White Men

The Indians had lived for thousands of years in America before the Europeans came. Like the ancestors of the Indians, these white men were not all alike nor did they all come at once.

As far as we know the first Europeans to come were the Vikings. The Vikings lived in Norway and parts of Iceland and Greenland. They were a seafaring people and great explorers. They sailed far and wide across the northern seas in their beautiful dragon ships.

The most famous of the Viking explorers was Leif Ericson. Nearly one thousand years ago, Leif Ericson sailed west from Greenland until he reached the shores of Canada. He did not know that he had discovered a new continent. He thought Canada was another island like Greenland. Other Vikings followed, but they did not stay, and finally ships from the Viking lands stopped coming altogether.

Two or three hundred years later, nobody is sure just when, other men came from Europe. At first *they* did not stay either. These men were fishermen. They came from England and France and Portugal to catch fish in the Gulf of St. Lawrence and off the coasts of Newfoundland.

They caught their fish and sailed home again without bothering to explore further.

Later, still other men came from Europe. At first they too did not stay. These men were not interested in fish. They were

looking for silk and spice. Silk and spice came from India and China and the lands of the Far East.

In those days people did not know as much about the world as we do. For instance no one in Europe knew about North and South America or the Pacific Ocean. They thought the world was much smaller than it really is. They thought India and China were on the other side of the Atlantic Ocean, quite close to Europe.

Christopher Columbus was the first explorer to sail across the Atlantic Ocean in search of these Far Eastern lands. In 1492 he set sail from Spain and after a long voyage landed on an island near the coast of South America. Christopher Columbus thought he had reached India!

Five years later, in 1497, John Cabot set sail from England. He, too, found land. He called *his* land The New Found Isle. We call it Newfoundland. John Cabot thought it was China!

After Christopher Columbus and John Cabot, many other explorers came to America, but, except for one man, none of them realized they had discovered an unknown part of the world. This one man was an Italian. His name was Amerigo Vespucci. Amerigo Vespucci said, "This is not China and it is not India. It is a whole New World."

Soon people in Europe began to give this New World a name. They called it AMERICA. And so, in the end, the new lands in the west were not named after Christopher Columbus, who first found them, but America, after Amerigo Vespucci, the man who knew what he had found!

In 1534 a French explorer, Jacques Cartier, came to New-foundland and sailed into the Gulf of St. Lawrence. He landed on the coast of Gaspé where he planted a cross and claimed all the land around and about for the King of France.

Jacques Cartier came back again the next year. This time he sailed around the Gaspé coast and explored the St. Lawrence River.

Jacques Cartier talked to the people he found living by the river, but he did not understand their language. He *thought* they said the name of their country was Kanada or Canada and so he, too, called it Canada. And CANADA it has been ever since.

The people by the river were, of course, Woodland Indians. The ones Jacques Cartier spoke to lived near the rock of Quebec. Québec is the way the French pronounced Kebec. Kebec is an Indian word meaning a narrow place. At Quebec the St. Lawrence River is very narrow.

Jacques Cartier left his ships at Quebec and went up the river in longboats.

Longboats are like large rowboats with sails.

After several days, Jacques Cartier came to a place in the river where the current was so swift the boats could go no farther. These swift currents were by a large island. There was a hill in the middle of the island and at the foot of the hill was an Indian village. The name of the village was HOCHELAGA.

The Indians at Hochelaga were very pleased to see Jacques

Cartier and his men. They danced and sang and gave them presents. Jacques Cartier read from the Bible. The Indians did not understand a word but they knew Jacques Cartier meant to be kind. When he finished reading, they took him to the top of their hill to see the view.

It was a very beautiful view of rivers and lakes and woods and hills; Jacques Cartier christened the hill Mont Réal or Royal Mountain. Nowadays there is no longer an Indian village at the foot of Mont Réal. There is a great city, and the name of the city comes from the name Jacques Cartier gave to the mountain—Mont Réal, or Montreal.

By the time Jacques Cartier returned to Quebec it was late in the fall. The trees were bare, there was frost on the ground and snow in the wind. Any day the river would fill with ice. Jacques Cartier knew the ice would crush his little ships and so he decided to spend the winter in Canada.

It was a terrible winter. The snows came early and it was bitterly cold. There was hardly any food. Even the Indians starved. Jacques Cartier's men fell sick and many died. In the spring the rest sailed back to France.

For a long time no other Frenchmen came to Canada. The French were busy fighting wars in Europe and had no time to explore.

But even though the French did not come back to the New World for a long time, there were other explorers who did—English and Spanish and Italian and Portuguese and Dutch.

Everybody wanted to go to America to find gold, or else to go to India and China to find silk and spice.

The people who were looking for gold, like the Spanish and Portuguese, went to South America.

The people who were looking for silk and spice, like the English and the Dutch, kept trying to find a sea route *through* North America. "There must be a passage from the Atlantic Ocean to the Pacific Ocean" they said. And so they kept sailing in and out of bays and up rivers and into inlets, wishing North America would get out of their way.

But North America just stayed where it was and the explorers went on and on and on.

New France

Then one day the French came again to Canada. The first man to do so was Samuel de Champlain, the Geographer of King Henry IV of France. In 1603 he crossed the Atlantic in his ship the *Bonne Renommée* and sailed up the St. Lawrence until he came to Tadoussac, at the mouth of the Saguenay River.

At Tadoussac Champlain and his men were welcomed by the Montagnais Indians who were having a feast. It was a victory feast because the Montagnais had just defeated the Iroquois.

At this time the Montagnais and all the other Algonkian people were at war with the Iroquois. The Montagnais were very pleased to have won a victory and they ate for days. Champlain asked the Montagnais if they and their Huron allies would like to have help in their war against the Iroquois. The Montagnais said "Yes." So Champlain said, "Good, my people will fight with your people against the Iroquois if your people will trade with my people and let us live in your country." The Montagnais said "Yes" again and so Champlain and his men sailed on up the St. Lawrence.

Champlain was delighted with Canada. He looked at the great trees and the rich black earth on the banks of the St. Lawrence River. He saw the wild fruits and berries and said, "This land is as good as the land of France. Frenchmen could live here very well."

Champlain went as far up the river as the Island of Montreal. There he looked for Hochelaga, but it had disappeared. There were no longer any Indians living on the island.

Champlain wanted to sail still farther up the river, but he couldn't because of the rapids. The Indians told him these were really very small rapids. "There are bigger ones," they said, "on the way to the Great Waters of the West."

Champlain became very excited. Surely the Great Waters of the West were the Pacific Ocean. He hurried back to France to tell the King.

The King and his ministers were delighted. They decided to build settlements in Canada. Then, after the North West

Passage was discovered, the French could trade with the Indians on their way to China.

The first French settlement was called Port Royal. It was close to where Annapolis Royal now stands in Nova Scotia. The French called Nova Scotia "Acadie" or Acadia. The settlers in Acadia had a terrible time. At first they were so cold and hungry they didn't care if anybody ever found the way to China, but they managed to build a fort and to plant seeds and grain and to stay alive.

In 1608 Champlain built another settlement. It stood beneath the great rock at Quebec. Champlain called it "The Habitation."

Samuel de Champlain was a wise man and a great leader. He helped the colonists to learn how to live in Canada and he governed them well.

Champlain was also a great explorer. Before he died at Quebec in 1635, he discovered Lake Champlain and explored the Ottawa River and some of the Great Lakes.

He was disappointed to find the Great Lakes were not the Pacific Ocean, but he was pleased with everything else.

Quebec

At Quebec the colonists planted gardens outside the walls of the habitation. Louis Hébert and his family were the first farmers.

Life was hard at Quebec. In summer, ships came from

France bringing food and supplies. But through the long, cold winter when the St. Lawrence was filled with ice there were no ships and no supplies. The colonists had to live as the Woodland Indians lived, hunting in the woods and fishing through the ice.

The French learned many things from the Indians. They learned how to make canoes and toboggans and how to use snowshoes and make maple sugar.

They learned how to find their way in the deep woods and along the waterways, and to hunt beavers. Everybody wanted to hunt beavers because they had such soft, thick fur. It was the kind of fur that made very good felt for hats.

In those days people in Europe loved to wear beaver hats. Gentlemen wore them decorated with great plumes. Ladies wore them in all shapes and sizes. Children wore them too.

And so the Indians hunted more and more beavers and bartered their fur to the French for knives and needles; for bright scarlet cloth and shining glass beads; for iron kettles and axes and GUNS.

The beavers escaped deeper and deeper into the northern woods and the hunters followed.

The Frenchmen who hunted in the woods with the Indians were called *coureurs de bois,* or runners of the woods.

By the time Champlain died many Frenchmen had come to live in Canada.

Soon the little habitation at Quebec grew until it was a town with churches and monasteries and a convent and a hospital and a Royal Governor and a Bishop.

The first Royal Governor to come to Canada was Count Frontenac.

Marie de l'Incarnation founded the first Ursuline school.

The first Bishop at Quebec was Monseigneur de Laval.

The priests and nuns who came to Quebec to look after the people in the colony took care of the sick and taught the children their lessons.

Missionaries were sent among the Indians. One of the best-known missionaries was Father Brébeuf. Father Brébeuf was as tall as a giant and had a giant's strength and courage.

But the Indians were not very interested in learning about Christ. "Christianity is all right for the French," they said, "but we are *another* people with different ways."

But the missionaries kept on trying and in the end many Indians became Christians.

The missionaries built their first missions by the Great Lakes in the land of the Huron people. These missions were really forts. Inside each fort was a chapel, a workshop, and a hospital. Outside the walls were the fields. The missionaries had to bring all their supplies from Quebec in canoes. They also brought chickens and pigs. It was very difficult to keep the animals in the canoes! It was even more difficult to move them over the portages!

A portage is a carrying place. Whenever a river was too swift or had too many rapids, a portage was made. To make a portage everything was taken out of the canoes and carried to the next place on the river where the waters were safe. The French word for carry is *porter* and that is why the French called these carrying places *portages*.

For many years the missionaries and *coureurs de bois* kept coming and going among the Indians. The missionaries did not like the *coureurs de bois* because they gave the Indians brandy in exchange for furs. Brandy made the Indians drunk and when the Indians were drunk they went wild and fought among themselves and did harm.

The Governor made laws to stop brandy being sold to the Indians, but many people broke the laws. This angered the Governor and the Bishop but they couldn't do much about it because the Pays d'en Haut, the Land Above, where the furs came from, was far away from Quebec, and many people were selfish and didn't care what happened to the Indians as long as they could get cheap beaver skins and make a lot of money.

The Pays d'en Haut, or Land Above, meant all the lands above and beyond the St. Lawrence valley.

More and more people kept coming from France. Soon there were settlements at Trois Rivières and Sorel and finally on the island of Montreal.

Ville Marie

The settlement on the island of Montreal was called Ville-Marie. Later its name was changed to Montreal. Ville-Marie was founded by Paul de Chomedey, Sieur de Maisonneuve. The first chapel and first houses and windmill and little hospital, where Mademoiselle Jeanne Mance cared for the sick, were built near what is now the harbour of Montreal.

But in 1642 when Ville-Marie was founded and the city of Montreal began, no ocean-going ships loaded and unloaded their cargoes on the docks. There were no docks, no ships, no cargoes, only a few men and women of great faith and courage who had come to found a town in honour of the Virgin Mary. That is why the first settlement was called Ville-Marie—the City of Mary.

Montreal began as a Christian mission but very soon it also became a trading post. Here, where the Ottawa and St. Lawrence rivers meet, came the Indians from the Pays d'en Haut with their furs. They traded their furs at a Fur Fair, which was held every year.

For several years all went well at Ville-Marie. Then sud-

denly a great fear fell on New France. The Iroquois were on the warpath!

It was rumoured they planned to attack the settlements on the St. Lawrence and drive the French from Canada. Why? Because the French were getting all the best furs from the Pays d'en Haut, and the Iroquois needed these furs to trade with the English and the Dutch who were settling in *their* part of the country.

Whenever the Iroquois tried to get furs from the Pays d'en Haut they were prevented by the Hurons and the French. The Iroquois decided to get rid of the Hurons and the French, and have all the good northern furs for themselves.

First they attacked and burned the Huron villages and destroyed all the French missions in Huronia. The Jesuit missionaries were tortured and killed. The Hurons who were still alive fled and took refuge with other tribes.

But this was not the end. There were still the French in Quebec and Trois Rivières and Montreal.

All through the winter of 1659–60 war parties gathered along the Richelieu and Ottawa rivers. The people trembled in their shoes. There were not enough soldiers or guns or ammunition. There was no time to send to France.

In the spring, while the little settlements on the St. Lawrence waited in fear, a never-to-be-forgotten fight took place on the Ottawa River.

One day in May 1660, Adam Dollard, a young officer from Montreal, and sixteen of his friends were attacked by the Iroquois at the bottom of the Long Sault Rapids on the

Ottawa River. Hastily Dollard and his companions and some Huron Indians who were with them took refuge in a nearby palisade.

Guns blazed, arrows sped, there were war whoops, shouts, and death. But despite the great number of Iroquois the fight was not soon over. For seven days and seven nights, with very little ammunition and without food or water, the French fought on.

Finally the Indians set the palisade on fire and Adam Dollard and the last of his companions were killed.

The Iroquois had won, but did they go on to Montreal and Trois Rivières and Quebec? They did not. Perhaps they decided if seventeen Frenchmen and a few Hurons could fight so bravely against such great odds it would be wiser not to attack the settlements on the St. Lawrence after all!

However everybody knew the Iroquois were still strong and New France would not be safe for long. Fortunately King Louis XIV decided to send soldiers from France to help the colonists. Their General was the Marquis de Tracy. The Marquis de Tracy and his men marched into the Iroquois country. Crops were burned, many villages destroyed, and the Iroquois forced to make peace.

Life in New France

Louis XIV did not just send soldiers to New France. He also sent new colonists. The colonists were encouraged to settle on the land instead of spending so much time travelling in the woods and on the waterways of the Pays d'en Haut.

Soon there were little farms all along the St. Lawrence River between Quebec and Montreal and down the Riche-lieu River as far as Lake Champlain.

Narrow fields ran back from the river so that the houses could be near to one another on the riverbanks. Before there were roads in Canada, the rivers were the highways.

The King granted land to seigneurs, or landlords, and they in turn granted land to the habitants, or settlers. The seigneur paid taxes to the King. The habitant paid taxes to his seigneur.

Wise men governed New France at this time. Many acres of land were cleared and farm animals were sent from France. The people were taught to spin and weave. They learned how to make tools and implements and to make their own furniture.

Forges to smelt iron were built on the St. Maurice River near Trois Rivières.

At Quebec there was a school for wood carvers.

The Ursuline nuns taught the girls of the colony to cook and sew and do fine embroidery.

Churches were built and in the churches were beautiful carvings made by the wood carvers at Quebec.

Many houses were built—low stone houses with high pitched roofs to shed the heavy winter snows.

More and more people came to New France.

French missionaries, explorers, and *coureurs de bois* went farther and farther across the country. They discovered vast lands and great rivers. Louis Jolliet and Father Marquette found the Ohio and Illinois Rivers. René Robert, Sieur de La Salle, who lived in Montreal, followed the great Mississippi River to the Gulf of Mexico. Pierre Radisson and Médard des Groseilliers, who came from Trois Rivières, explored the lands above the Great Lakes toward Hudson Bay.

One day Pierre Radisson and Médard des Groseilliers had an idea. Instead of making the long, hard, dangerous journey by canoe from Quebec or Trois Rivières or Montreal to

get furs in the Pays d'en Haut, and then having to turn round and go all the way back again to Montreal, why not send the furs by ship from Hudson Bay?

There were no finer furs in North America than the furs to be found in the lands around Hudson Bay.

"It will be quicker this way," they told the Governor at Quebec, "and much, much cheaper."

But the Governor did not think so and besides he disliked Radisson and Groseilliers because they sometimes traded without a license and so he said "No."

Radisson and Groseilliers got very angry. In a huff they went to France. In France the King said "No" too. That made them so angry they went to England. The merchants

in London did not say "No." They liked Radisson and Groseilliers very much. They found their names hard to pronounce so they called them Mr. Radishes and Mr. Gooseberry. They thought Mr. Radishes and Mr. Gooseberry had a very good idea indeed and so they formed a company. They gave this company a very long, high-sounding name, The Governor and Company of Adventurers of England Trading into Hudson's Bay. Most people just called it the Hudson's Bay Company.

In 1671 the company began building trading posts on the shores of Hudson Bay. This worried the people in New France because now there were English to the north as well as to the south. The Governor of New France and the French King wished they hadn't said "No" to Mr. Radishes and Mr. Gooseberry, but it was too late. The English were already on Hudson Bay and Hudson Bay was near the best fur country in North America.

Meanwhile the colonists in New England were worrying about the *French.* New France was not only growing bigger, but the French were exploring far and wide and claiming all the lands they found for the King of France. In fact the French were going so far and claiming so much that the English began to wonder if there would be any land left for them in the West! Would they have to live along the Atlantic coast *forever?* The English didn't like *this* idea at all.

For a time all was well and then fighting began and there was no peace anywhere.

Pierre d'Iberville, who was the greatest soldier in New

France, attacked the English forts on Hudson Bay and the English settlements in Newfoundland.

In 1690 the English colonists sent two expeditions against New France, one by sea, one by land. The land expedition got lost but the sea expedition sailed up the St. Lawrence and attacked Quebec.

Admiral Phipps, the English Commander, sent a messenger to Count Frontenac, the French Governor. "You must surrender," the messenger said.

But Count Frontenac wasn't going to be pushed about by the English. "I will answer your commander with the mouths of my cannon," he shouted, and told the messenger to be gone.

The English ships bombarded Quebec. From the heights of Quebec Count Frontenac's cannon bombarded the English ships. Admiral Phipps looked up at the great rock with its blazing guns. "It is no use," he said. "Quebec is too strong," and he sailed away.

Meantime the English had been stirring up the Iroquois. The Iroquois began raiding New France again. At Lachine, near Montreal, there was a massacre. At Verchères a young girl called Madeleine and her two little brothers had to defend their father's fort against the Iroquois for days. Finally they were rescued by soldiers from Montreal.

In New England people were afraid to go to bed in case a raiding party of French and Indians would creep out of the woods and set fire to their houses and burn them alive, or scalp them if they tried to escape.

In New France people trembled when they thought of Lachine. Every farm became a fort. Nobody was safe anywhere.

In these raids there was nothing to choose between French and English. Each side was as bad as the other, which is generally what happens when people start fighting.

At last in 1697 France and England signed a peace and for the time being the fighting was over.

The Indians also signed a peace. This happened at Montreal in 1701.

From Quebec came the Governor and all the French officers in their splendid uniforms, and from the lands around and about came the Indian chiefs in their ceremonial robes.

Everybody made long speeches and smoked the peace pipe and gave each other presents and then went happily home.

The peace between the French and Indians lasted, but *not* the peace between England and France. From 1702 to 1713 again there was war. At the end of this war Acadia was ceded to England and for more than forty years there was no fighting to speak of in North America.

During these years the French went on exploring. A fur trader from Trois Rivières, Pierre de la Vérendrye, and his sons, went far out across the Prairies and built trading posts on the Saskatchewan River.

The La Vérendryes persuaded the Plains Indians to trade with them instead of making the long journey to Hudson Bay to trade with the English. This made the English angry.

As a matter of fact everybody was beginning to get angry all over again. The English were mad because the French in Acadia wouldn't swear loyalty to the English King and because the French in the St. Lawrence valley were getting all the best furs. The French were mad because people from New England were beginning to push West into lands round the Ohio River. The French had already explored these lands and they did not feel the English had any right to them. Everybody knew there would be war again.

In 1721 the French had built a fortress on Cape Breton Island. It was called Louisbourg. There was a fine harbour at Louisbourg. Here ships from the French fleet could have a base near the mouth of the St. Lawrence River. Once Louisbourg had been built the French felt Quebec and the other settlements on the St. Lawrence could be more easily guarded.

Not to be outdone the English finally built a naval base of their own in Nova Scotia. It was called Halifax. Halifax was begun in 1749.

Shortly after Halifax was built, the English Commander decided if there was going to be war then the Acadians had better be moved out of Nova Scotia.

There were many people in the American colonies who thought this was a good idea, especially the people in Massachusetts. "The Acadians may not be warlike themselves," they said, "but they incite the Indians to attack us. It will be safer if they are out of the way."

Nobody in England knew about the Commander's plan.

Nobody in Acadia knew either, until one Sunday ships
filled with soldiers came to the little settlements on the
Acadian coast. The soldiers went on shore and rounded up
the people like cattle and forced them on board the ships.
Then the ships sailed away to settle the Acadians in other
British colonies far away from Canada. The Acadians suffered

very much. Even the ones who escaped and made their way to Quebec were not treated very well. Life is never easy for refugees.

Many people in England were angry when they learned what had happened to the Acadians, but it was too late to do anything about it.

Later the laws were changed and some Acadians came back, but Acadia was no longer their home. Settlers from New England had rushed in and taken over their farms. The Acadians were now strangers in their own land.

This is a cruel story, like most stories of war and the things that happen because of war.

How New France Became Part of British North America

In 1756, after the exile of the Acadians, the war everybody had been expecting began. It is called the Seven Years War. The Seven Years War was fought between England and France in Europe and Asia, as well as in North America.

From France the King sent the Marquis de Montcalm to command his armies. Unfortunately the Marquis de Montcalm and the Governor, the Marquis de Vaudreuil, did not get along very well. This made things difficult.

The British had their difficulties too. Their generals were not very clever and the American colonists were *very* stubborn.

The colonists wanted to fight the war one way and the British wanted to fight it another. Everybody started arguing and while they argued one battle after another was lost.

First they were beaten by the Marquis de Montcalm at Fort Oswego on Lake Ontario, and then at Fort Ticonderoga on Lake Champlain.

William Pitt, the British Minister of War, decided something had to be done.

He appointed new generals and made Lord Amherst Commander-in-Chief. He also promoted new officers in the Navy.

The British had the most powerful navy in the world. They had many more ships than the French. Because of this the British were able to capture Louisbourg.

Once the British had captured Louisbourg there was nothing to stop the British Navy sailing into the Gulf of the St. Lawrence and up the river to Quebec. Matters began to look bad for the French.

Unfortunately at this time there were some very dishonest men in the government at Quebec. They broke the laws and robbed and cheated the people in order to make money for themselves. They did not care if the people starved and the British won the war.

The Marquis de Montcalm was in despair. He sent to France for help but little came and in the spring of 1759, as soon as the ice was out of the St. Lawrence, the British Navy sailed up the river and laid siege to Quebec.

Admiral Sir Charles Saunders was in command of the Navy.

Major General James Wolfe was in command of the Army.

All summer the siege went on.

The British camped on the shores opposite Quebec. Day after day their cannon bombarded the town. Churches and buildings were destroyed and many people were killed.

From the ramparts of Quebec the French fired back at the British ships but they could not sink them and the ships kept on sailing up and down in front of the town.

When was General Wolfe going to attack? Where were the British troops going to land?

Some thought below the city and some above.

The summer wore on. "How can we make the French surrender?" the British asked, and they began burning villages and destroying crops all along the St. Lawrence River. In terror the people fled into the woods. But General Montcalm and the French Canadians refused to surrender. "This is our land," they said, "we will not give it up."

It was a hot, damp summer. Day after day the sun blazed down. There were terrible thunderstorms. In the British camps men fell sick. Mosquitoes buzzed and bit. At night Indians prowled about and scalped the British sentries at their posts.

Would this dreadful war never end? The summer days dragged on and then at last it was fall.

The night of September 12–13 was very dark. There was no moon. In the early hours of the morning of September 13 the British troops began landing on the north shore of the river above Quebec.

Quickly they climbed the cliffs and overcame the French sentries at the top. By the time the sun was up, General Wolfe's army was on the Plains of Abraham, outside the walls of Quebec.

The French could not believe their eyes! *"Les anglais sont arrivés,"* they said. "The English are here." Word was sent to the Marquis de Montcalm on the other side of the city. Hastily he marched his army back to Quebec and out onto the Plains of Abraham.

The Marquis de Montcalm rode at the head of his troops. There were French Canadians and Indians and a few regiments from France.

Many of the French Canadian soldiers were farmers and

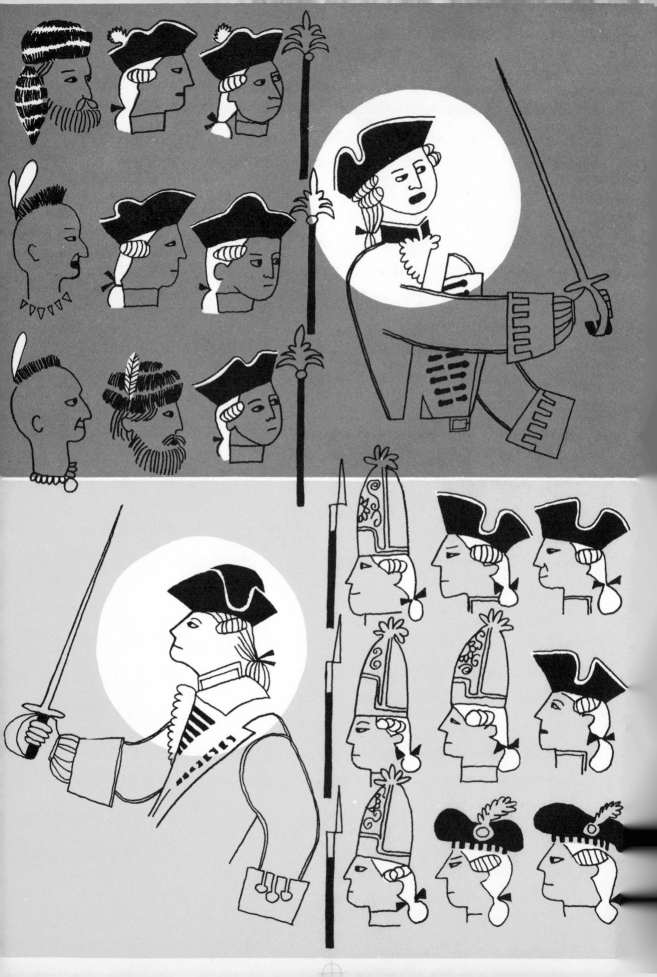

coureurs de bois who fought better in the woods than on a battlefield.

The British waited until the French were only forty paces away. Then they split the air with a mighty volley. The French lines halted and broke. There was furious fighting. Within little more than an hour the battle was over. General Wolfe was dead and the Marquis de Montcalm mortally wounded.

Three days later Quebec surrendered.

But there was still Montreal.

All winter the British guarded Quebec and the French Montreal. Then in the spring the French, under the Duc de Lévis, made their way down the ice-filled river and over the frozen fields to Quebec. They hoped to recapture the city, and they very nearly did! There was another great battle on the Plains of Abraham and this time the French won.

But the gallant Duc de Lévis did not have enough men and guns to capture the city, and so he camped his army outside the walls and waited for help.

The British inside Quebec were also waiting for help. Whoever got it first would win the war.

Everbody looked down the St. Lawrence for sight of a sail. At last a ship was sighted.

All eyes were on her as she sailed into Quebec. Was she French or British? Suddenly a flag broke from her masthead and all who looked could see it was the British flag. The Duc de Lévis and his men were forced to retreat up the river to Montreal.

That summer three British armies marched against Montreal: one from Quebec; one from New York; and one from Lake Ontario down the St. Lawrence. By September they had reached the island of Montreal and surrounded the city.

There was nothing for the French to do but surrender. And so, on September 8, 1760, the Marquis de Vaudreuil handed Montreal over to Lord Amherst. The Seven Years War in America was over. New France was now part of British North America and for a few years New York and Boston and Philadelphia and Quebec and Trois Rivières and Montreal all belonged to Britain.

These years were difficult for the Canadians. It is always hateful to live under enemy rule. The British tried to govern well. They let the Canadians keep their religion and their language and many of their laws, but it was not a happy time for anybody.

However a few years later, in 1776, when the thirteen American colonies rebelled against Britain because they wanted to govern themselves, the Canadians did not join in the revolt.

The Americans sent armies into Canada. One army captured Montreal and another besieged Quebec, but the Canadians refused to have anything to do with the American Revolution, and in the end the Americans were driven away and Canada remained British.

When the American colonies won their independence from Britain, they joined together and became the United States of America.

Loyalists

In the American colonies there had been many people who did not want a revolution. They were called LOYALISTS because they remained loyal to Britain.

When the Revolution was over and the American colonies became the United States of America, many of these people were driven from their homes. Others were thrown into prison. Some were killed.

"Let us escape," the Loyalists said, "to lands where we can still live under the British flag." And so they packed up their belongings and left the United States.

Many came to Canada.

They came by sea and they came by land.

They settled in Nova Scotia and in what later became New Brunswick and on the shores of the St. Lawrence River above Montreal. Hundreds also settled in the Niagara peninsula and by the shores of Lake Ontario.

The King rewarded their loyalty by granting them land and giving them money and supplies, but it was difficult for them to start life all over again in the wilds of Canada.

The coming of the Loyalists brought great changes to Canada. Now there were many people who spoke English and were Protestant as well as people who spoke French and belonged to the Roman Catholic Church.

Both people were used to different ways of believing and

thinking and living and it was not easy for them to get along together.

Because it was not easy for the French and English to live together, the British Government decided to divide Canada into two parts—Upper Canada and Lower Canada.

When this was done in 1791 it made six colonies: Upper Canada, which is now Ontario; Lower Canada, which is now Quebec; Nova Scotia; New Brunswick; Prince Edward Island; and Newfoundland.

These colonies were known as British North America. In each colony there was a lieutenant governor and a council and an assembly.

The first lieutenant governor of Upper Canada was Lieutenant Colonel John Graves Simcoe. He did a great deal for

his province. He built Fort York, which later became Toronto, and offered free land to new settlers.

Many new settlers came from the United States. These new settlers were not like the Loyalists. They did not care which country they lived in so long as the land was free.

Life on the frontier was hard. There were no towns, no roads, not even fields. Nothing but the rivers and lakes and endless forest.

The first thing a settler had to do was cut down trees and build a house. Generally this house was a one-room log cabin with a fireplace. The fireplace heated the cabin. It was also used as a stove.

Once he had built a house the settler had to clear his

land. With only an axe it takes time to cut down trees. The settler had to cut down hundreds and hundreds of trees before he had enough land to plant his crops.

When the trees were cut they were burned. The land between the stumps was ploughed and the settler planted his grain. The settler had only a wooden plough and handmade rakes and hoes. He had to plant his grain by hand. When the grain was ripe he had to cut it and thresh it by hand.

Until there were mills the settler also had to grind his own grain. This was done by pounding the grain in a hollow stump with a wooden pestle. It took a long time to grind enough grain to make flour for a loaf of bread.

The settler not only had to clear his land and build his buildings, but he had to make many of his tools and most of his furniture. His wife had to spin and weave and sew. She also had to make soap and candles. Sometimes she taught the children their lessons because at first there were no schools on the frontier and if children did not learn to read and write at home, they did not learn at all.

As time went on and more and more settlers came, there were roads and towns and villages, and the land began to look as it does today.

But in the beginning this was not so. The life of the pioneers in Nova Scotia and New Brunswick and Upper Canada was lonely and hard and dangerous, just as it had been once for the pioneers in New France. It took strong people to live on the Canadian frontiers and make a country out of the wilderness.

Lords of the Lakes and Forests

Not all the settlers in Canada worked at clearing the land and making farms. Many preferred the life of the woods. These men were fur traders and explorers. From Montreal the traders and explorers of the North West Company went across the prairies. They built trading posts as far out as the foothills of the Rocky Mountains and in the lands that lie toward Hudson Bay.

There was great rivalry between the Nor'westers, as the traders of the North West Company were called, and the traders of the Hudson's Bay Company.

Some of the North West Company partners stayed in Montreal to look after stores and supplies and to ship the furs to England. Others went out to the lonely trading posts in the Pays d'en Haut and spent the winters collecting furs from the Indians.

Every spring supplies were sent by canoe from Lachine on the St. Lawrence River near Montreal to Fort William at the head of the Great Lakes. Every spring furs were shipped down to Fort William from the trading posts in the West.

At Fort William the furs were loaded into the canoes from Montreal and the supplies that had come from Montreal were loaded into the canoes from the West, and after a few days of feasting and merrymaking the fur traders started out again on their long, hard journeys.

The canoes travelled very fast. They were paddled by men called *voyageurs*. The *voyageurs,* like the *coureurs de bois* of an earlier day, preferred life in the woods to life in the settlements. The *voyageurs* were magnificent canoemen. As they paddled they sang. They sang many songs we still love to sing. *"En roulant ma boule roulant"* and *"Alouette gentille alouette"* and *"Au clair de la lune"* and many more.

The *voyageurs* were as brave as they were strong. They had to be, to paddle their canoes in dangerous waters and to carry furs and supplies over the portages.

Among the fur traders in the North West Company there were famous explorers—Alexander Mackenzie, Simon Fraser, and David Thompson.

Alexander Mackenzie discovered the Mackenzie River and followed it all the way to the Arctic Ocean. Two years later he went across the prairies to the Rocky Mountains and over the Rocky Mountains to the Pacific Ocean. When he reached the ocean he wrote his name and the date on a rock in Bella Coola Bay. The rock is still there and on it is written: "Alexander Mackenzie, from Canada, by land, the twenty-second of July, one thousand seven hundred and ninety-three."

A few years later Simon Fraser discovered the Fraser River. With his *voyageurs* he travelled down its rushing, swirling waters to the Pacific Ocean.

David Thompson explored the Rocky Mountains and made a map of all the lands in the North West. He had only simple instruments but he made a very accurate map. Nowadays people know David Thompson was one of the greatest geographers of all time.

Meantime, fur traders from the Hudson's Bay Company were also exploring.

Sometime before Alexander Mackenzie discovered the Mackenzie River, Anthony Henday travelled from Hudson Bay to the foothills of the Rocky Mountains. He spent the winter there among the Blackfoot Indians and was probably the first white man to see the Rockies.

Another Hudson's Bay trader, Samuel Hearne, discovered Great Slave Lake. He went from the Churchill River to the Coppermine River and followed the Coppermine to the Arctic Ocean.

It was not long until other fur traders followed Alexander Mackenzie and David Thompson and Simon Fraser over the Rocky Mountains to the Pacific Ocean.

This meant that men were now travelling from Montreal to the Pacific Ocean by *canoe*.

As time went on, more and more trading posts were built in the North West. They were built by both the North West Company and the Hudson's Bay Company. Sometimes the posts were built quite close together.

There was always trouble between the fur traders. Every trader wanted the best and cheapest furs for his own company and often there were brawls and men were killed.

1812

For many years there was peace in Canada, while people went on clearing the land and building farms and working in the fur trade. Then once again there was war.

War with the United States!

Today, this seems very strange because the United States and Canada have been friends and have lived peacefully together for many, many years.

In 1812 it was different. There were lots of United Empire Loyalists in Canada who still hated the United States, and in the United States there were many people who were angry because Canada hadn't joined the American Revolution. There were also American settlers who very much wanted the rich lands of Upper Canada for themselves.

Still there might not have been war if Britain and France hadn't been fighting each other in Europe.

This war made things difficult for the United States because the British Navy tried to prevent all trading ships getting to Europe. The Americans bought and sold a lot of goods in Europe. When their ships were captured they were angry.

The British said they were sorry, but that they were fighting for their lives against the French and their Emperor Napoleon and they had to do everything they could to win the war.

The Americans said, "We will not stand for our ships being stopped. The seas are free," and declared war on Britain.

Some Americans got very excited. "Now we can conquer Canada," they said "*That* will fix Britain and then we won't have to argue any more about *who* owns *what* in North America." Other Americans, especially the people in New England, thought the idea of conquering Canada was stupid. They refused to have anything to do with the war.

But there was war just the same!

The war was fought on the Great Lakes, along the St. Lawrence River, and on the Atlantic Ocean. There were many land battles beside lake battles and sea battles. Sometimes one side won and sometimes the other.

The two best-known soldiers on the Canadian side were General Sir Isaac Brock and Colonel Charles d'Irumberry de Salaberry.

General Brock was killed while leading his troops at the Battle of Queenston Heights on the Niagara River.

Colonel de Salaberry and the French Canadians won a victory at Châteauguay and prevented the Americans from capturing Montreal.

But perhaps the two people we hear most about are the Indian Chief Tecumseh and Laura Secord, the wife of a Canadian soldier.

Tecumseh was a Shawnee. The Shawnees were Woodland people who lived near Lake Michigan. The Americans, who were settling that part of the country, had been waging war against the Shawnees and driving them from their hunting grounds. The Shawnees hated the Americans for this and so they decided to help General Brock.

Tecumseh was killed in the fighting but he was a fearless warrior and he and his people gave General Brock much help.

Laura Secord helped in a different way. One day she slipped past the American lines and went alone through the great, dark woods near Queenston to warn the British and Canadian troops that the Americans were hiding nearby, waiting to attack.

There were wolves in the woods and rattlesnakes. Many times Laura Secord lost her way, but she struggled on until she found the soldiers and delivered her message. It was a very brave thing for her to do.

The War of 1812 went on for two years. The Americans kept on trying to cross the border and capture Canada and the Canadians kept on pushing them back.

At last Britain and her allies defeated the Emperor Napoleon. Britain stopped fighting France and the United States stopped fighting Britain and trying to conquer Canada, and so the Canadians were able to stop fighting the United States and get back to work.

The worst thing about the War of 1812 was that it left Canadians and Americans disliking each other. People who live next door to each other *have* to be good neighbours. Fortunately, as time went on, Canadians and Americans learned how to live together. Often, even today, they do not agree, but they are friends and find it very silly to think they once were enemies.

The Red River Colony

One day just before the War of 1812, a rumour raced through the Pays d'en Haut. It was said that a Scottish lord, the Earl of Selkirk, had bought a huge tract of land from the Hudson's Bay Company.

What was Lord Selkirk planning to do with this land? It was said he planned to bring settlers from Scotland.

Settlers? The North West Company traders were frightened and angry. The Plains Indians would have been angry and frightened too, if they had known what it was all about.

Farms in the middle of the buffalo country! If this happened the buffalo would wander away. Buffalo cannot live like cows in a field. They need great spaces in which to graze.

If these things came about, what would become of the fur

trade? How could anybody in the West live without buffalo? It was not only the Plains Indians who depended on the buffalo for food and clothing. So did the Nor'westers and the Métis.

The Métis were half Indian and half European. They lived near the forts and worked for the fur traders.

All these people needed pemmican for food. Without buffalo there would be no pemmican.

There was a terrible to-do. The North West Company tried to stop Lord Selkirk and his settlers, but the Hudson's Bay Company encouraged them and in 1811 the first ones arrived. They came by way of Hudson Bay and settled on the Red River, below Fort Garry, which is now Winnipeg.

The Selkirk settlers had a frightful time. They did not have proper tools to build their houses or enough supplies to last until they could grow their own food. The Nor'westers and the Métis made trouble for them at every turn. There were skirmishes and fights. People were killed. The whole Red River was thrown into an uproar. The fur trade looked as if it might be ruined. However before this happened the North West Company and the Hudson's Bay Company agreed to stop fighting and join together. The new company that they made kept the old name of the Hudson's Bay Company.

Once the North West Company became part of the Hudson's Bay Company, Montreal was no longer the centre of the fur trade. The furs were shipped to England direct from Hudson Bay.

New People and New Ways of Living

But it was not only the ways of the fur trade that changed at the beginning of the nineteenth century. Almost *everything* in Canada changed.

New settlers came in larger and larger numbers. In spite of the War of 1812, some even came from the United States! But most of them came from Great Britain. With the coming of these new people, new industries began. No longer were furs the only things men bought and sold.

In Lower Canada lumbering became important. As the land was cleared the trees were cut into logs and floated down the rivers to Quebec. Here the timber was shipped to Britain.

There was also lumbering in Upper Canada and in Nova Scotia and New Brunswick. In Nova Scotia and New Brunswick there were many shipyards, especially in Nova Scotia, which became famous for her sailing ships.

Now there were lumberjacks and raftsmen on the rivers as well as *voyageurs*. The lumberjacks were the men who went into the woods and cut the trees. The raftsmen were the men who drove the logs down the rushing rivers.

These men were hardy and daring. Like the *voyageurs,* they loved the wild, carefree life of the woods and rivers.

Potash

Not all the timber was sent down the rivers. Often when the settlers cut down trees they had to burn logs and brush before they could plough the land. When they did this they gathered the wood ashes and boiled them with lye in great iron pots. This made potash.

Potash was used for bleaching cotton and making soft soap. It was one of the first things the settlers had to sell.

Bees

Sometimes it was impossible for a man to clear his land or gather his crops all by himself so his neighbours would give him a hand.

When people gathered together to help one another in this way, they said they were having a BEE.

There were all of kinds of bees. Logging bees and husking bees and sewing bees and barn-raising bees and, of course, sugaring bees.

The sugaring bees were in the spring when the sap began to run and everybody went to the sugarbush to tap the maple trees. A sugarbush is a wood where sugar maples grow.

All through the warm spring days and the cold spring nights, the maple sap dripped into wooden buckets hanging on the trees.

When the buckets were full, the sap was poured into large pails or barrels and taken to the sugarhouse where it was boiled until it thickened into syrup.

Some of the maple syrup was made into sugar. Maple sugar, maple syrup, and wild honey were often the only sweetening the early settlers had.

Travel

As time went on, life became easier in the Canadian colonies. Roads were built. These roads were very rough but they made it possible for people to move about and keep in touch with each other.

Carts and coaches travelled on the roads as well as men on horseback. It took many hours to go short distances and often travellers got sick from the rocking and rolling of the coaches.

In winter when there was lots of snow on the ground all was well, but during the rest of the year the roads turned into bogs when it rained and the carts and carriages got stuck in the mud.

The lakes and streams and rivers were still the best "roads," but people were beginning to settle farther and farther inland and could no longer go everywhere they wanted in canoes.

In time there were canals. These were built to bypass the

many rapids on the St. Lawrence and Ottawa rivers. You can portage a canoe, but not a boat, and certainly not a steamboat!

The first steamboat in Canada, and one of the first in the world, belonged to a Montreal merchant, John Molson. It was called *The Accommodation* and it ran between Montreal and Quebec. Its speed was four miles an hour, which was very fast indeed for the year 1809.

But most of the river traffic was still done in Bateaux and in Durham Boats. The Bateaux were made in Quebec. They were wide boats with a square sail. When a Bateau reached the rapids it was dragged upstream by its crew or by a team of oxen on the riverbank. This was called tracking.

Durham Boats were larger than Bateaux. They had a round bow and were steered by a rudder.

In the West they used York Boats, which were long and flat-bottomed and could be dragged over the portages. They could also be poled upstream, or tracked by men or oxen along the shore.

In the West there were no roads. When people travelled across the prairies they used Red River Carts. These carts had only two wheels and were made entirely of wood.

Everywhere there were rafts.

Rafts were made by lashing logs together. Often the raftsmen built shacks on the rafts for their families.

The first railway in Canada was built in 1836. It ran between Laprairie, across the river from Montreal, and St. Johns, a small town on the Richelieu River near the United

States border. The early trains ran only in summer. They had to stop when the snows came. Later they ran all year round.

Soon there were railways between Montreal and Toronto and between Montreal and the seaport of Portland in the United States.

In time there were railway lines connecting many towns in New Brunswick and Nova Scotia as well as towns in Upper and Lower Canada.

The coming of the railways brought great changes to the people in the Canadian colonies. Now it was easier to travel long distances and get from place to place.

Besides steam locomotives there were also steamships. The first steamships had sails as well as engines. Later they managed without sails. The first steamship to cross the Atlantic Ocean without sails was the *Royal William*. The *Royal William* was built in Quebec in 1833.

Rebellion of 1837

While all these things were happening, a good deal of talking had been going on in the colonies. The talking was about politics. Many people in Canada did not like the way Britain governed the colonies. They felt they did not have enough say in making the laws under which they lived.

They asked that the laws be changed. When they weren't, a number of people in Upper and Lower Canada rebelled.

The leaders of this rebellion were William Lyon Mackenzie and Louis Joseph Papineau.

There was fighting between rebels and government troops outside Toronto and in villages near Montreal, but the rebellion failed. It failed because most of the people who wanted the laws changed wished to do things in a more peaceful and lawful manner.

After the fighting was over, the British Government sent Lord Durham to find out what the Canadians really wanted. He travelled around the country and talked to fishermen and farmers and lumberjacks, as well as to businessmen and government officials. When he had done this, he wrote a report.

This report is known as the Durham Report. In it Lord Durham said that people in Canada did not want to break away from the British Empire and form a new nation as the United States had done. He said Canadians were happy to be part of the British Empire, but they wanted the right to govern themselves.

When this was understood in Great Britain certain laws were changed so that Canadians could have more say in their own affairs.

About this time a little lumbering village on the Ottawa River was chosen to be the capital of Upper and Lower Canada. It was called Bytown. After Bytown became the capital, its name was changed to Ottawa.

Confederation

A few years after these events, sometime around the middle of last century, people started talking about joining *all* the Canadian colonies together to make one large country like the United States. This was known as Confederation. Confederation comes from a Latin word that means to unite or join together.

Not everybody in the colonies thought this was a good idea. But the people who believed in Confederation said, "As separate colonies we are weak. If we join together, we will be strong. Unless we are strong, we will never be able to govern ourselves, or stand up for our rights, or be independent from the United States."

The more people thought about this, the better they liked the idea of Confederation.

Soon leaders from all the colonies began meeting to make plans for Confederation. The most important of these leaders were Sir John A. Macdonald from Upper Canada, Sir George Etienne Cartier from Lower Canada, Sir Leonard Tilley from New Brunswick and Sir Charles Tupper from Nova Scotia.

There was a great deal of arguing and chopping and changing, which always has to happen if people with different ideas are to agree about anything.

When everybody *had* finally agreed, an act was passed by the British Parliament. This act was called the British North America Act.

On July 1, 1867, the British North America Act became law and Nova Scotia and New Brunswick and Lower Canada and Upper Canada became the Dominion of Canada.

These four colonies were now provinces. Lower Canada became the province of Quebec, Upper Canada became the province of Ontario, and Nova Scotia and New Brunswick became provinces too.

Sir John A. Macdonald and all the men who made the plans for Confederation are called the Fathers of Confederation. A motto was chosen for the new Dominion of Canada.

A MARI USQUE AD MARE

The meaning of the Latin is "from sea even unto sea."

The Fathers of Confederation dreamed of a country that one day would stretch all the way from the shores of the Atlantic Ocean to the shores of the Pacific Ocean. But on July 1, 1867, the Dominion of Canada only stretched from the Atlantic Ocean to the Great Lakes. It did not include either Newfoundland or Prince Edward Island, which at the last moment decided not to become part of Canada after all.

But after many years, the dream of the Fathers of Confederation came true. First Prince Edward Island joined the Confederation and then British Columbia and in 1949, Newfoundland at last changed its mind and became a province too.

The Settling of the West

For as long as they could, the fur traders prevented anybody from settling on the prairies. But as more and more people came to live in Canada, even the Hudson's Bay Company could not stop settlers from moving into the West.

Soon there were other farms on the prairies besides the farms on the Red River.

With the coming of these new settlers, there was trouble, just as there had once been trouble about Lord Selkirk's settlers.

As they watched more and more of the prairie land being turned into farms, the Plains Indians and the Métis grew frightened and angry, especially the Métis. "How are we to live?" they cried. "Where can we hunt? Where are we to go? What will become of us?"

The leader of the Métis was Louis Riel. Louis Riel was half Indian and half French and like all the other Métis he wanted his people to be free to follow the ways of their ancestors.

"We want our own colony," Louis Riel told the government at Ottawa, "and our own laws."

But the government did not listen to Riel and so the Métis rose in rebellion.

Soldiers were sent out to the Red River and the rebellion was put down. Afterwards the Canadian Government bought all the land that had once belonged to the Hudson's Bay Company. Some of this land was made into the province of Manitoba. The rest was known as the North West Territories. The Hudson's Bay Company was allowed to keep its fur trading posts in the North West Territories, but it was no longer ruler of the land.

The North West Territories stretched all the way from Manitoba to the Rocky Mountains and from the American border to the Arctic Ocean.

To keep order in these vast lands, the government formed the North West Mounted Police. Later they became known as The Royal Canadian Mounted Police. The men who belong to this force are known as "The Mounties." The Mounties are one of the most famous police forces in the world.

Because they were brave and just, The Mounties were respected by the Indians and by the settlers who came to live in the North West Territories.

Nowadays The Mounties are the police of the government of Canada and of most of the provinces.

The first rebellion of the Métis happened in 1869–70. There was a second rebellion in 1885 because the Métis were still very unhappy about the way they were being treated by the Canadian Government. The Plains Indians were also unhappy about what was happening to them and so some of them rose in rebellion with the Métis.

The Métis and the Plains Indians had many reasons to be unhappy, but whether they were right or wrong they could not be allowed to take up arms against the government. Rebellion means the end of law and order. Without law and order a country falls apart.

Once again soldiers were sent to the West and once again the rebellion was put down. Many people still argue about the rights and wrongs of this rebellion.

After the North West Rebellion, large tracts of land were put aside for the Métis and the Plains Indians. This land was known as the Indian Reserves. The Métis and Plains Indians did not like the idea of living on Reserves, but the government persuaded them it would be better for them to do so and in the end they agreed. On the Reserves the Indians and Métis were allowed to live according to their custom, but it was not the same. No longer were they able to hunt buffalo on the prairies they loved. By 1875 the buffalo were disappearing and the old way of life was changing for the Plains Indians just as it was for Indians everywhere in North America.

The Canadian Pacific

Even with Confederation Canada might never have become a nation had it not been for the railways. Particularly if it had not been for the Canadian Pacific Railway.

This railway was started a few years after Confederation.

It was the first railway to be built across Canada. It took men of imagination and courage to build it.

For months and years engineers and workmen struggled to lay tracks through the forests of northern Ontario and around the lakes and over the swamps that lie between the Great Lakes and the Red River. The tracks kept sinking in the swamps. In one place several lots of track sank before the engineers found firm ground. The work was easier on the Prairies. But then there were the Rockies! Here, tunnels had to be blasted through the mountains and bridges built across the rivers.

In 1885 the last track was laid, the railway was finished, and Canadians could go by train from coast to coast.

More New Canadians

Once the C.P.R. was built settlers started moving into the North West Territories. Many of these settlers came from other parts of Canada and from the United States, but most of them were Europeans.

They came from many countries: from Poland and Germany and Italy and Norway and Sweden and Holland as well as from England and Scotland and Ireland and Wales.

These people came because they felt they could make a better life for themselves in a growing country.

The journey from Europe was a hard one. It still took many days to cross the Atlantic Ocean. Often the immigrants were crowded into dirty, leaky ships. Because of dirt and crowding and bad food, many of them died before they reached Canada.

But despite the hardships, people kept coming, for in Canada the laws were the same for rich and poor and every man had a chance to get ahead, and all men were free.

New towns sprang up in the North West Territories: Regina, Moose Jaw, Calgary, Prince Albert, Edmonton, Swift Current, Medicine Hat. . . . Soon there were so many people that the Canadian Government decided to make two new provinces.

In 1905 the land that lies next to Manitoba became the province of Saskatchewan and the land between Saskatchewan and the Rocky Mountains became the province of Alberta.

At first farmers in the West grew many crops and kept different animals just like farmers in the East. Then they discovered the prairie was a wonderful place for wheat. Soon everbody in Manitoba and Saskatchewan was growing wheat.

In Alberta they grew wheat too, but there were also cattle ranches. Once again great herds roamed on the western plains, but herds of beef cattle instead of herds of buffalo. By this time nearly all the buffalo had been killed by the settlers.

The New People of the Pacific Coast

Beyond Alberta lies British Columbia. The first Europeans to come to British Columbia were sailors and explorers like

Captain Cook and Captain Vancouver. Later there were fishermen and fur traders. The first fur traders came by sea. There was no Panama Canal in those days so they had to sail around South America.

Then in 1793 Alexander Mackenzie came all the way across Canada by land. Other fur traders followed in his footsteps. Soon there were trading posts and forts in the Rocky Mountains and along the Pacific coast.

For many years the people in British Columbia were mostly fishermen, fur traders, and lumbermen. Then one day in the 1850s GOLD was found in the mountains. Prospectors and miners rushed into British Columbia from here, there, and everywhere. Mining camps sprang up over night. The whole colony was in an uproar.

Some of the prospectors and miners found gold and became rich. Some found gold and lost it and were as poor as ever. Others found nothing at all.

When the gold rush was over, many of the people who had come in search of gold stayed and settled in the mountain valleys and by the sea and turned their attention to lumbering and fruit farming and other things.

British Columbia was so far away from the eastern provinces that for a time some people thought it might be better for the colony to join the United States. However, when they heard there was to be a railway they changed their minds and decided to become part of the Dominion of Canada.

O Canada

And so at the beginning of the twentieth century the Dominion of Canada really did stretch from sea to sea.

In the twentieth century, the century you and I are living in, many changes have taken place in Canada.

Not only gold but copper, silver, iron, nickel, coal, bauxite, and uranium have been found in the rocks, and under the prairie wheat fields men have discovered oil.

Montreal and Toronto and Winnipeg and Vancouver have grown into great cities.

There are eighteen million people living in cities and on farms and ranches and in towns and villages from the Niagara peninsula to the arctic seas and from Prince Edward Island to the Yukon.

How amazed the early fishermen from Europe would be

if they could see Newfoundland now with its great power dams and paper mills.

What would Jacques Cartier and Champlain think of New Brunswick and Nova Scotia and Quebec with their mines and factories and electric power?

What would the Loyalists think of Ontario, and Governor Simcoe of Toronto?

What would the La Vérendryes and Alexander Mackenzie and David Thompson say if they could see the Prairies now with giant machines cutting the wheat, and oil wells pumping night and day?

What would Captain Vancouver think if he could see the seaport city that bears his name?

How La Salle and Jolliet and Father Marquette would marvel to see the St. Lawrence Seaway taking ocean-going ships right up the river past the falls and rapids to the head of the Great Lakes.

What would all these men think if they knew we now fly in hours over distances that took them months and years.

How different they would find it, these people who came to Canada long ago. And yet they would find many things that had not changed.

There are still the great rivers and lakes and mountains and the cold arctic seas. There are still forests, though not the forests they knew. There are still the rolling prairies and the great skies and the silence of empty spaces.

The Canada they knew is still here—a land of hope where men are free.

Index